Additional print and eBook copies can be purchased through Amazon.
Library and Archives Canada Cataloguing in Publication
ISBN: book: 978-1-987990-05-8
        e-book: 978-1-987990-04-1
Bedwin, Christa, 1974 –, author
Client-Pleasing Reports & Communications: A Workbook / Christa Bedwin

**SOLA
ROSA**

This book was produced by Sola Rosa Publishing.
Our mission is to publish only books that help people feel good or help them live
better.

Layout: Raaj Chandran

Reviewers:
Many engineers, scientists, and language experts have reviewed this document and
participated in the seminar, adding their wisdom and experience to it over the years.

This seminar has visited at least 12 cities in 3 countries so far and is revised as
colleagues make suggestions for improvement.

Thank you to all the senior colleagues who have shared their wisdom and
experience. in the creation of this document, and to all the junior colleagues who
have been brave and committed enough to ask questions.

Special thanks to Marcel Chichak, Les Sawatsky, Patricia McIsaac, and Patsy Price for
their mentorship, patience, encouragement, and support.

Client-Pleasing
Reports & Communications:
A Workbook

CHRISTA BEDWIN
B. Ed., B.Sc., CYT

SOLA
ROSA

1. **When you first sit down to write, think of your reader.**

2. **Be committed to giving them an excellent experience.**

3. **If the reader did not understand, you did not communicate.**

This book is dedicated

to every engineer, scientist, business writer, or student

who routinely **stops to think**

if they can present their ideas better;

to every person brave enough to ask questions;

and to every mentor who takes the time to help others improve.

Preface

This document was born through working with thousands of engineers and scientists world-wide, from fresh-from-university new hires to 35-year-plus veterans. My industry experience also includes working with scientific researchers from all over the world.

Some of them were native English speakers from a variety of countries (England, Australia, New Zealand, India, Singapore, the US, and Canada), while others spoke several other languages before English (French, Spanish, Farsi, Portuguese, Arabic, Chinese, Japanese, German, and many more).

I interviewed, and was approached with questions by, hundreds of engineers, scientists, and others about the challenges they have with reporting and communicating.

This is the advice that the senior folks would like the junior folks to know about writing reports and communications for clients.

If you have any questions or would like to suggest additions, I would love to hear from you through my LinkedIn account or e-mail me at christabedwin@gmail.com.

Sincerely,

Christa Bedwin
April 2015

References and Resources

References typically occur at the back of a report. They appear first in this book, because to learn to write reports within a company structure you must align your practices with the company practices and resources.

New university graduates need to learn how to write for clients instead of their professors. People who come from other companies need to learn the procedures and styles that have been set within the new company.

Large companies often have templates and style guides. Seek those out. Sometimes it can require digging because a lot of people are unaware that they exist, but chances are that some caring person at some point has made such a guide. A consistent guide is essential to produce professional-quality communications, and following consistent guidelines improves the collective work environment for all.

1. Dictionaries

Groups should agree to be consistent with spellings from one standard dictionary to reduce conflict and increase quality.

Normally, use spellings for the destination country of the report or document (where the client is, or sometimes where the site is). I suggest:

- The Canadian Oxford Dictionary for Canada

- The Oxford English Dictionary for the UK, Europe, Africa, and Asia

- Merriam-Webster's Dictionary for the US, http://www.merriam-webster.com/

- The MacQuarie Dictionary for Australia, https://www.macquariedictionary.com.au/

There may be some cases where there are compelling reasons (e.g. a strong client preference) to deviate from the standard dictionary spelling for certain words. If so, these deviations must be properly agreed upon, documented, and well-communicated to everyone concerned through a style sheet.

Premium Tip

Rebels Without a Cause

Problems arise when individuals choose their own deviations from the standard spellings and styles, often with no apparent rhyme or reason. These trivialities eat up everyone's time in exponential ways. Be clear, consistent, concise, and collegial.

2. Style Guides

Style guides reduce conflict by offering standard use of punctuation, grammar, and capitalization. Usually companies set smaller style guides that contain just the information relevant to their company or certain projects. These guides are, or should be, based on broadly accepted standards. The most popular and accepted style guides for science, engineering, and business are:

- The Chicago Manual of Style: http://www.chicagomanualofstyle.org

- The Canadian Style Online: http://btb.termiumplus.gc.ca/ tcdnstyl-srch?lang=eng&srchtxt=si%20units&cur=5&nmbr=18&lettr=&page=

- Scientific Style and Format (the Council of Science Editors) http://www.scientificstyleandformat.org/

3. Metric Guidelines:

Bureau International des Poids et Mesures http://www.bipm.org/en/si/

National Institute of Standards and Technology http://physics.nist.gov/cuu/pdf/sp811.pdf

4. References

This book includes excerpts, with permission, from the references below.

- *The Subtleties of Scientific Style* by awesome Aussie Matthew Stevens. A fun-to-read, but serious scientific style guide. You can obtain this book as a free pdf and pay by donation at http://www.ung.si/~sstanic/teaching/CIS/Stevens-Subtleties_of_ Scientific_Style.pdf

- *Eight Step Editing* by Jim Taylor (That book is available now only to seminar participants in the Editors' Association of Canada course, Eight Step Editing. However a similar book is available for sale: *Quick Fixes For Business Writing* by Jim Taylor, ISBN 978-1-55270-252-9, 2006.)

CONTENTS

WRITING IS ALL ABOUT YOUR AUDIENCE

After you have put together all your science and calculations for a project, the first thing you need to do when you sit down to write a report is think:

Who is reading your document?

If you are writing an academic article for an engineering research journal, then you can use things like the following without needing to explain anything:

- complicated technical terms

- scientific notation

- units written technically such as 6.112×10^3 mh^{-1}

However, if you use language or mathematical symbols that are unfamiliar to your clients or readers such as regulatory personnel or the public, it does not make you look smarter. It just makes them feel confused. Think about your audience and decide if it would be better to write 6.112×10^3 mh^{-1} or 6 000 m/h or 6 km/h.

Attitude Adjustment

People who arrive in industry straight out of university need to learn a new way of communicating and writing. In M.Sc. and Ph.D. programs, particularly, we learn to use large words to impress our professors and others in our field.

In industry, when you are dealing with clients, you need to learn to do the opposite – speak and write as simply as possible. It is not a matter of dumbing anything down. It is just a matter of writing and speaking as simply as possible.

There is another kind of adjustment needed every time you change companies. To succeed, find out the procedures and styles of reporting in your new company. Talk to people at various levels to find out what they need from you given your job role In the reporting hierarchy and how to work well within the team.

Premium Tip

Make Your Reader Feel Brilliant

Smart business people learn to make their clients feel smart, rather than trying to appear smart themselves. Clients who find it easy to understand you will be happy and confident that they know what you are doing for them, and why, and how. They will be repeat clients, and will recommend you to others.

Exercise 1

1. Describe the characteristics of typical readers of each kind of communication:

Document Type	Typical Reader Characteristics
Proposals	
Environmental Assessments	
Technical Memos	
Client Reports	

2. Who might your secondary readers be? Think of at least three categories of people. These are people who you might not have planned to have read your communications, but who might end up reading them, either immediately or far into the future. What would the motives of those people likely be?

Secondary Reader Type	Motivation to Read Your Report

LEAD WITH STRENGTH: INTRODUCE YOUR DOCUMENT WELL

Exercise 2

What do you do when you pick up a report with no introduction? Describe your actual movements and actions.

A good introduction welcomes the reader in. It makes them feel like they comfortably know the path you are going to lead them down and they can clearly see where they are going to go next, and where they might jump to if they wanted a particular kind of information about your report.

There are three pieces that help to introduce a document. They are:

The Executive Summary

This piece must be written last, when you know the subject matter really well. The executive summary must perfectly encapsulate the essence of the rest of the report. Some people, especially more senior people in positions of authority, may only read this part of your report. Polish it well.

The Table of Contents

The table of contents is an excellent place for a reader to introduce themselves to the contents of the report. It makes a small executive summary all on its own, telling readers what sections you have deemed most important by the headings you use and the numbers of pages that you invest in each.

The Table of Contents might be thought of as a road map to the report.

The Introduction

The introduction should include all of the "5Ws and the H."

Exercise 3

1. Write the 5Ws and the H here.

2. Then write an example introduction to a report that includes details to cover all of those

categories.

ORGANIZATION & SIGNPOSTING

Signposting is a word that means you lead your reader through your report so that they never feel lost. Whenever they come to a fork in the road, they feel clear about where they are going and why they are reading this.

Just like a road map and road signs help you navigate when you are on a car journey, the signals you give in how you organize your documents help your readers navigate.

When you are organizing your report in preparation for writing it, put the signs on your road map first. Colouring in the roads with detail can happen second.

There are a few very useful tools for signposting a report well.

- headings
- tables of contents

Headings

Make sure that your headings reflect the content of each section. Make them descriptive, but concise.

Premium Tip

Clear Headings

Acronyms should not appear in headings or titles. The reason for this is that you can not expect people who first pick up your report to know your acronyms. Those people will often skim the table of contents and the titles before they read the text where you first explain the meaning of each acronym.

Therefore, titles with acronyms in them present a cloud – they leave unknowns in the table of contents and the headers. Spell them out instead of leaving a cloud.

How to Organize a Consulting Report

Here are five methods that other consultants have suggested to decide on the original road map of organization for a new report.

Take a broad view: If you have a lot of data or ideas to present (for example, a large new environmental assessment) and you are not sure how best to organize it:

- Gather all of your information together in a hard format of some kind – even if all you have to start with is headings or ideas on cue cards.
- Get into a board room with a big table, and lay out what you have (each bit on a separate paper).
- Rearrange it until you see a way for it to make sense.
- This method is particularly great for large team projects.

Bullet point method

- Set up a table of contents and a rough outline before writing.
- Bulleted paragraph-by-paragraph or sentence-by-sentence outlinesfor each section can be rearranged easily at this stage.
- Then go write to flesh out your outline with proper sentences and paragraphs.

Like a research paper or lab report: A good client report may be very similar to the lab reports.

- What were you asked to do?   (Intro)
- What did you do?   (Methods)
- What did you find?   (Results)
- What do you think about what you found?   (Discussion)
- What does this mean for your client?   (Conclusion)

An existing example:

Many companies have past reports that you can refer to. Just ask your supervisor for a past report that is similar to the one you need to do, and see if the table of contents suits your purposes. Feel free to improve on the past reports! However, If you cut and paste any parts of a previous report, do it paragraph by paragraph, reading carefully to make sure that each piece of information is still relevant.

Also make sure that you have copyright permission to do this.

Template tools

Making a "skeleton document" from a template is a great way to get over writer's block. Enter in the titles, create a table of contents, and then you'll find that you do know how to start filling in some of the sections under some of the titles. Start, then chip away at the easy bits, then the next easiest, and the next, until you finish.

After you have organized the skeleton or road map of your report, then and only then are you ready to start writing paragraphs.

Read on for some ways to do this in the most readable way possible, and a couple of ways that people have really failed.

Premium Tip

Check Your Report Balance and Get Some Encouragment with the Table of Contents Feature

1. Write your document. Use the heading style option in Word to mark your headings. You can also use second and third level headings.

2. Under references in the Word menu, ask it to insert the table of contents. (Note: You might have started with a good table of contents but redo it to check along the way for how you are doing with balance. It is very encouragin to see the page numbers climb as you fill in the pieces.

3. Scan the table of contents to check if you have organized your material so that equal-importance topics have equal heading levels. It should read like a clear and logical road map to your document and almost tell the story of your report itself.

4. Now scan the numbers of pages that you have assigned to each section. Is your content balanced, or do some sections need bulking up, and others need paring down?

Example: Unbalanced Passion from a Numeric Modeller

There once was a young numeric modeller who had to report to the client about the modelling work that he had done.

He spent 12 pages explaining why he used the modelling program that he had used, and comparing it to other inferior (in his opinion) programs.

He explained in great detail the variables he chose to represent the variable factors on the physical site.He included mathematical explanations.

And then he included a half a page answering the question the client asked in the first place. It did not look very client-focussed. It came across as very unbalanced. Clients want to feel cared for. Consider their needs and desires first when you start writing.

Lesson: It's easy and fun to geek out on the math and science, but gauge whether your client will enjoy that or be frustrated. Many of our clients are not as mathematically inclined as we are and will have difficulty wading through such explanations, or, they might be too busy to read all that right now. Try to shift the balance to factors they are more interested in reading about, and never waste their time.

PACING – KEEP YOUR READERS AWAKE AND ENGAGED

A document with many long, elaborate words, long, elaborate sentences, and long, unbroken paragraphs is HARD TO READ. (By the way, so are obnoxious words all in capitals! Avoid both.) You want your reports to be easy for your clients and fellow scientists and engineers to read and scan.

Here are some tips. How could you improve these sentences?

1. Short words are easier and quicker to read than long ones, and short sentences are easier and faster to read. The brain processes them faster.

2. Long sentences tend to be more laborious; the brain needs to hold data from each part of the sentence while processing additional data, which is a long and difficult process compared to the way it digests a collection of short sentences.

3. Semi-colons can often be replaced by periods; this makes shorter, easier sentences.

4. Short paragraphs tend to have just one idea in each. This makes the ideas in a report faster and easier to digest.

5. Making more paragraph breaks also creates more white space on the page. This makes reading easier on the eye and brain.

6. Double negatives are not just long, they are also not always easy to untangle, so do not use them. (Anyway, it's more powerful to word things positively.)

Premium Tip

Yes, What You Just Read Was Garbage, I Agree!
This page has been deliberately written badly. If you have not noticed that it's a terrible mess, then you are not paying very good attention! Please edit this page as you look at it. Some suggestions for improvements follow on the next page.

Exercise 4

1. What is the difference between the first and second point?

2. Why leave white space instead of a solid block of text?

3. Why use bulleted or numbred lists

4. How do you make shorter sentences?

Possible Answers: Better Tips.

1. Short words and short sentences are easier and quicker to read. The brain processes them faster.

2. Long sentences tend to be more laborious. The brain needs to hold data from each part of the sentence while processing additional data, which is a long and difficult process compared to the way it digests a collection of short sentences.

3. Semi-colons can often be replaced by periods. This makes shorter, easier sentences.

4. Short paragraphs tend to have just one idea in each. This makes the ideas in a report faster and easier to digest.

5. Making more paragraph breaks also creates more white space on the page. This makes reading easier on the eye and brain.

6. Double negatives use more words than required and are difficult to untangle. Do not use them. It is more powerful to word things positively.

Premium Tip

Shortening Words By Any Means Possible?

What about contractions (such as don't, it's, we're)? Is that a good way to shorten words?

No. Contractions are not a good way to make shorter words in formal writing. Spelling words out is almost always clearer, and contractions are usually frowned upon in formal English writing.

Shorten your text only to help make it more readable. It doesn't make sense to shorten it, then don't. There is no point to saving space if it makes your writing harder to understand.

Article: How Long Should a Paragraph Be?

You do not eat a big chunk of roast beef whole. You slice it up. Think about the digestibility of your ideas the same way. Do you have a little chicken drumstick of an idea, or a whole roast beef?

You would never serve your guests a roast beef without slicing it. Do not serve meaty, weighty ideas without slicing them up, either.

Over my decades of editing I have heard plenty of "rules" about paragraphs, usually going back to things that school teachers said to young children in a desperate attempt to get more words out of their little hands. These false ideas include:

- WRONG   Paragraphs need a beginning, middle, and end.
- WRONG   Paragraphs must be at least three sentences.
- WRONG   Repeat your topic sentence at the end.

None of those are true for adult writing, and particularly not in the internet age.

Redefine what you think paragraph breaks are. Try this idea:

"Paragraph breaks are a way to create white space surrounding your important ideas."

If you write something that is not important, well, can you delete it? If not, then it can go in the middle of a paragraph. But your important ideas should show up at the beginning of paragraphs.

Readers now skim the first lines. That's how we do it now that we are used to the internet. If you bury something in the middle of a paragraph, it probably will not get read.

So please do not write long, heavy paragraphs. Slice them up!

This is essential for technical reports, because you need your clients to access your important points, and the faster they can do that, the happier they will be with you.

By the way, this is also true of modern novels. I can tell a self-published novel these days by (among other things) the lengths of the paragraphs – most fiction readers these days are not willing to wade through Dickensian twelve-sentence paragraphs. And why should we? Make the read more pleasurable by breaking things up. (Aside: If you are going to self-publish and not hire an editor, consider at least comparing your novel to published novels that you enjoy, to learn how to improve your own. Copy their strategies.)

Experiment for yourself. Take a look at some of your favourite new reads and compare them to something old – huge difference. In medieval times, monks could sit quietly reading with no distractions, and sentences averaged 82 words. Now, we are constantly distracted in our reading, and sentences average 8 words.

The way you use your white space on the page, and your paragraph and sentence length, affect comprehension.

Remember that.

Article: The Best Ways to Punctuate Bulleted Lists

Bulleted lists are a fantastic way to present parallel information. Compared to straight paragraphs:

- They are many times faster to read.
- They are many times faster to understand.
- It is easier to remember the information presented in a list.
- They are very easy to locate when returning to the report.

There are two considerations that people use when they are trying to decide how to punctuate bulleted lists:

- readability considerations
- company policies and style guide

Frequently, the company policy is based on historical practice. Therefore, you will see many large corporations (including governments) that insist on a semi-colon after each point. Their logic will go something like this:

- that is how our founders did it;
- that is how it taught was in the style guide in their day; and
- if it was good enough for them, then it's good enough for us.

Modern readability research has taught us a few things that suggest changes to that old style, such as:

- People are able to read more quickly and easily if you remove the extra clutter.
- The bullet points are enough punctuation on their own, without a semi-colon on the end.
- People are able to process ideas most easily if they are delivered in complete sentences.

For lists of simpler concepts, don't use any punctuation at all. For example, this list is:

- si ple
- naked
- readable

What about capitalization?

- Capitalize items that are full sentences.
- Do not capitalize items that are simple words or phrases.

Other things you should know about bulleted lists:

- Limit lists to 7 items. If you have a list longer than that, break it into two or more lists by better categorizing the items.
- If you will need to discuss items in a list with another party, consider numbering the list instead of just using bullets.
- If the list has an order (such as a procedure), use numbers instead of bullets.

Exercise 5

In case of fire, notify the switchboard of the fire's location, leave the build –ing immediately, using the stairs - do not use the elevators, or you may end up trapped between floors if electrical power is cut off, either by the

fire or as a safety measure, while the unobstructed vertical shaft attracts heat and smoke like a natural chimney – direct the spray from fire hoses at the base of the flame, but do not return to the building until instructed to do so.

- based on a variety of observed notices

1. What is wrong with this? (Plenty.)

2. Now, say the #1 thing that is wrong with it.

3. Fix it. Rewrite here.

INNOVATE: THE SHAPE OF WHAT YOU PRESENT MATTERS

As we have said, a wall of dry text is not that pleasant to read. Think of the shape of your text and what you can do to break things up. Also, think outside the box to find innovative ways to present material other than paragraph after paragraph after paragraph.

This improves the look of your report, and more, it can radically improve your message.

Here are three innovative communication suggestions that have worked well In their contexts. What other ways might you innovate? If you take some time to apply your creativity outside the standard boxes, you may find all kinds of interesting solutions. Use a PowerPoint format? Present the client with a video message? The sky is the limit if you are willing to engage your powerful mind.

- boxes
- magazines
- photos

Write the method used in the example below.

Method: _____

Example: Comparing Many Factors

An engineer was asked to present a comparison of water treatment technologies for a mining operation. She had five different technologies to present, and the client wanted to know pricing, environmental impact, staffing, and operational factors for each one. The table of contents alone for this written as a report would have taken two or three pages. There was the potential for a lot of repeated boilerplate text and headings.

Instead, we changed the format completely and visualized a larger, poster-size piece of paper. We put the five technologies across the top in a table format, and put the various factors the client needed to know about in rows down the side.

We filled in the boxes with short summaries of the details the client needed to know for each one. When more supporting information was needed than could fit in the table cell, we referenced pages later in the report.

Aside from being fewer words, this format allowed everyone to see the project options at a glance, and compare the methods much more clearly than they could have done flipping back and forth in standard report pages.

Think Like a Magazine Designer

Reports that read like web pages or magazines also make for an easier reading experience than old-style paragraph-after-paragraph reports. Now I am not saying to use photos of gorgeous people and glossy paper. But think about how the words flow.

How can you make the writing more magazine-fast to read? Use more frequent headers to give the readers signposts regarding the content inside.

Think of it the same way you would if you are on a long drive through the country. If you see signposts now and then, you know you are getting somewhere. If you don't see any road signs, you can't feel sure where you are until you see a landmark or a sign. Give your readers these signs frequently.

> Another interesting technique that is not in most engineering report templates, but which might be applicable for you, is to use margin boxes or pull quotes. These can effectively highlight the text.

Some of you may respond that you just pull out your GPS or telephone to see where you are – your readers can't do that. Make sure you equip them. You put in the GPS signals. Lead them comfortably along the adventure trail that is your report.

Premium Tip

Clear Safety

People in emergency situations are not going to stop to read essays. Safety documents must be concise, fast, and clear to read, and formatting is essential. The fire notice in Exercise 5 needs to be trimmed extensively and re-worded as a quick-access list.

Bulleted or numbered lists or information in table format are excellent presentations for safety material. Another excellent format in some cases may be to use an illustration.

Klaus Hofer, safety and literacy researcher, suggests using a question and answer format. The safety reader approaches a text with a question (e.g. "what do I do when there is a fire?") A safety document must provide quick to read answers and no extra words. For example:

In case of fire:

- Notify the switchboard of the fire's location.
- Leave the building immediately.
- Do not use the elevator.
- Use the stairs.
- Gather outside at the designated area.
- Do not return to the building until directed to do so.

Write the method that should have been used in the example below.

Method: _____

Then write three lessons that you can learn from this group's mistakes to avoid making this mistake in the future.

1.

2.

3.

Example: New Technology

I was working with an engineering team once that had spent twenty or twenty-five pages describing some new technology options for horizontal drilling in the oil sands to a client. After reading ten pages of this (they had struggled hard to write it, and I struggled hard to read it), I finally got up out of my desk and walked over and asked, "what does this machine that you are talking about, look like? And do you have some images of the various brands you discuss here that we could show the client?"

By using a photo, or, even better, a labelled diagram, of each technology, they could have saved 8 pages of writing for each one. It is likely that the vendor of each multi-million-dollar instrument would have gladly provided such a diagram. Then, a comparison chart with the costs, benefits, and disadvantages of each one would also have been appropriate.

Unfortunately, this tale has a sad ending. The team had not sought any editing until the last day of a three-week writing process, and they sent the whole sorry mess off to the client because they did not think there was time to fix it. Though editing could improve the English, what would have profoundly made this better would have been a complete restructure at the beginning. A larger-view edit.

Lesson 1: Think about how you are going to present your information by drawing the road map and thinking about what you are presenting to the client before you start to colour in the detail on the roads between your road signs.

Instead of defining some clear roads to walk the reader along, this team just started writing. They waded in and started struggling, and they made a horrible experience for their readers.

Lesson 2: Check in with your reviewers at earlier stages in long projects. If you leave it until the last minute, they may not be able to offer much help.

Lesson 3: If someone comes along with an idea to reduce the number of words you have written, do not be afraid to hand over the golden scissors. Everyone knows that it is difficult to delete words that you wrote yourself, especially when you struggled for hours or days to write them. **But your product is not your words.**

Your product is your message, and your solid science, engineering, and business thought.

Use a Picture

Procedures can be well served by using images. Look at this example from the Cenovus web site. Instead of wading through a page full of paragraphs, we know at a glance what this page is about, even without wading through the paragraphs. The paragraphs are essentially there to remind us of any steps in this SAGD process we can't remember.

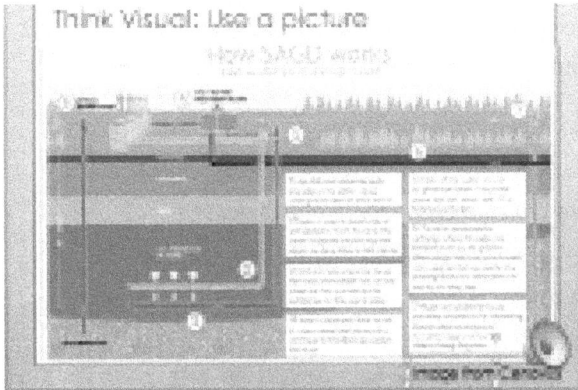

Exercise 6

Some people in the office wrote up a field safety guide for operators to use in the field. The guide was about the safety checks that all need to be done when using the company pickup trucks. They formatted it as 21 bullet points and squished it a bit to make sure it all fit on one page. Ack!!

Even if it was made into 21 numbered points, nobody can reasonably be expected to learn and memorize 21 points.

At most, a bulletted list should have seven points. If a list has more, it must be broken up into categories so the reader can reasonably sort and understand the information.

So that is a minimum change before it goes out to the field. Maybe the list could be broken into 5 points to check about the tires, 6 to check about the engine, 3 to check about the lights, and so on. But what is an even better solution? Think of one or two and describe, draw, or write them here.

TECHNICAL REPORTS ARE THE OPPOSITE OF MYSTERY NOVELS: USE ACTIVE VOICE, NOT PASSIVE

Popular author Stephen King has given some great advice in his book *On Writing: A Memoir of the Craft.* (http://www.westga.edu/~jloicano/Stephen_King_Passive.pdf) He says:

> "*One of my pet peeves has to do with the most basic level of writing, and I want to get it off my chest... Verbs come in two types, active and passive.*
>
> *With an active verb, the subject of the sentence is doing something. With a passive verb, something is being done to the subject of the sentence. The subject is just letting it happen. You should avoid the passive voice.*
>
> *How about this:*
>
> ***My first kiss will be recalled by me as how my romance with Shayna was begun.***
>
> *Oh, man, who farted, right? A simpler way to express this idea – sweeter and more forceful, as well – might be this:*
>
> ***My romance with Shayna began with our first kiss.***
>
> ***I'll never forget it.***
>
> *I won't say there's no place for the passive tense.*
>
> *Suppose, for instance, a fellow dies in the kitchen but ends up somewhere else.* ***The body was carried from the kitchen and placed on the parlor sofa,*** *is a fair way to put this.*"

(Ed: especially if it's a murder mystery when we don't know who did it!)

Since you do know, presumably, who did the work for the science in your report, there is no need to write it as if the actor is unknown. Do not write technical reports as if they are murder mysteries. Write them as if you are the detective who knows it all at the end of the show:

> *Sam and Ella carried the body from the kitchen and placed it on the sofa.*
>
> *Our field team tested all 12 boreholes on the Morengi site on Tuesday, March 6, 2015.*
>
> *I kissed her and I'll never forget it.*

Premium Tip

No Doubt
Remember your kisses, reveal the murderers, and leave your readers in absolutely no doubt as to who did what. If you want to write mystery stories, do that after work.

Are you accountable for your work? Did you do a great job?

It is easy, especially when you have read too much of it, to fall into a habit of writing everything in the passive voice in a completely unaccountable way.

The passive voice is useful when you do not know who is acting. It is particularly useful if there are legal reasons that you do not want to take accountability for something.

However, writing in the passive voice has **three distinct disadvantages**:

- It uses many more words.
- It makes the document harder to read.
- It obscures accountability.

If your team did the work, say so, proudly. Instead of saying, "the work was done," say, "We did the work." This helps to build the client relationship.

In the last half-century, there are many projects have been passed between various consulting companies. When the reports are written about these projects, built on past data, and everyone for two decades has used some stiffly formal passive voice, it becomes nearly impossible to untangle who has done what.

If you are not comfortable saying "we did it," you can say "our company did it."

Exercise 7

Passive language keeps us at arm's length from the people we are writing to, and obscures accountability. Practise rewriting the following sentences in the active tense, and add a personal touch at the same time.

Passive	Active
1. Your cheque will be mailed by the accountant.	
2. Your contribution to the church lunch was appreciated.	Thank you for bringing cookies to the church lunch. I noticed the ladies' table particularly gobbled them up with great delight. (You make it more personal, and you don't even have to say that you loved them yourself!)
3. The budget has been approved by the client.	
4. The field work will be done.	

The excerpt on the following two pages is a fun read directly quoted from Matthew Stevens' book *The Subtleties of Scientific Style*. (I messed up the formatting, with persmission.)

This excerpt is included for your amusement and thoughtful pondering. It also provides a large text that illustrates the effects of formatting. See Exercise 8 at the end.

" "We have all read sentences like, "It is concluded that Pqr1 mediates the daylength response in petunia," or "It is thought that this result was due to contamination."

But "it is thought," "it is concluded," and the like are **weasel words**. ["Statements that are intentionally evasive or misleading" *Concise Oxford Dictionary*. See also Watson's *Dictionary of Weasel Words* (Watson 2004).]

They allow the author to slip out of the reader's grasp. The reader can't answer the question "Who thinks it?" or "Who believes it?" because the author has sidestepped the issue.

Fowler (*Modern English Usage*) wrote that use of the third person "often amounts to a pusillanimous shrinking from responsibility … The person addressed has a right to know who it is that entertains a feeling he may not share or a thought he may consider mistaken, and is justly resentful of the suggestion that it exists in the void."

There can be many reasons why authors might use this construction:

1. **They don't know who thinks it but don't want to admit it.** This is sloppy scholarship. If a fact cannot be verified, it is no more useful than hearsay. If it's important enough to be used in an argument, then it's important enough to verify.

2. **They can't be bothered looking it up.** More sloppy scholarship.

3. **They don't want to admit that they think it** for fear that it won't sound important or reliable enough. This stems from the belief that "science is objective" (see below), or that their opinion doesn't count as much as someone else's.

4. **They are unsure about the conclusion and want some wiggle room** in case it turns out to be wrong. Again, sloppy scholarship. If the data are clear, then the conclusion is clear. If the data are unclear, then say so.

5. **That's how they learned it as students.** Old habits die hard, and are often passed on to the next generation.

6. **"That's the way reputable journals do it."** Maybe some do, but many don't (including *Nature*, Oxford University Press and *Behavioral Ecology*, to name a random few found in a Google search). The best example I can give is the paper that formed the foundation of all modern genetics:

    ### A Structure for Deoxyribose Nucleic Acid

    We wish to suggest a structure for the salt of deoxyribose nucleic acid (D.N.A.). This structure has novel features that are of considerable biological interest.

    A structure for nucleic acid has already been proposed by Pauling and Corey. They kindly made their manuscript available to us in advance of publication. Their model consists of three intertwined chains, with the phosphates near the fibre axis, and the bases on the outside. In our opinion, this structure is unsatisfactory for two reasons:

    (1) We believe that the material which gives the X-ray diagrams is the salt, not the free acid. Without the acidic hydrogen atoms it is not clear what forces would hold the structure together, especially as the negatively charged phosphates near the axis will repel each other.

    (2) Some of the van der Waals distances appear to be too small.

    (Watson JD, Crick FHC. 1953. Nature 171: 737–738.)

7. **"Because science is objective."** Let's get this straight: Science is **not** objective.

Perhaps the social construction theorists have gone a bit far in their analyses, but they are certainly right about one thing: science is a product of the human mind. My mind is subjective. So is yours. So is that of any scientist who formulates hypotheses, prepares tests, thinks about results, and draws conclusions. Every step in the process of science takes place in someone's mind and is subject to all the inexactnesses and the conscious and unconscious biases that are the product of that finite organ. We perceive the world through the lens of our own training and upbringing, culture, experience, beliefs, knowledge and expectations. The world might be "out there," but the only way we can interpret it is subjectively. We can argue that a thermometer is objective. It's an inanimate object that responds according to the laws of physics to its surroundings. So if I tell you that the temperature is 25°C, you and I have the same understanding of the temperature. Nevertheless, you might perceive it differently from me. I could say "that's pleasant," but you could say "it's hot today." Our interpretations differ. Even the assumption that temperature is important could be a bias: relative humidity might be more important.

As Albert Einstein showed with his special theory of relativity, our points of view matter.

And as Niels Bohr showed us through quantum physics, even the act of observing can determine the outcome.

"OK," you might argue, "science **ought** to be objective."

But if it were, it would not be science. We would call it religion, and find our truths carved in slabs of stone, immutable. Science is a process. It is an intellectual activity. Until we meet another civilisation from the stars, we have to assume that it is solely a human activity. No other species practises it; it doesn't just happen. "Well," you persist, "should we even bother to attain objectivity?" To this the answer is a clear yes. Objectivity is like absolute zero. Just because it can never be reached is not a reason to ignore it, and cool (!) things like superconductivity can be achieved by striving. Objectivity is the unreachable, but often visible, boundary that defines our subjectivity. It is essential in science—indeed, in rational living—to acknowledge our subjectivity and the spin it puts on our interpretation of facts. We should always aim for objectivity, in the way that Buddhism aims for perfection, even though we know we can never reach it. As long as we acknowledge our subjectivity, we have a functioning science. Why? Because we can test things indifferent ways (triangulate) to confirm our belief, and can make the effort to explicitly state our assumptions so that we can challenge each one before we proceed. So to come back to the reason for this diatribe, we cannot write "It is observed that …" on the basis that science is objective, because it isn't.

The observer matters. There are several reasons for writing science in the first person. By acknowledging the people involved, the author:

- makes the article more accessible to the reader (turns a one-way lecture into an implicit dialogue)
- lets the reader know exactly who did the work (the active voice is an important part of this, identifying the actor)
- takes credit for the work
- accepts responsibility for the work.

In removing themselves from the story, the authors imply that they cannot be held responsible for the work. But the corollary is that they are not responsible for any kudos – something no researcher would accept."

The excerpt on the past two pages is a fun read directly quoted from Matthew Stevens' book *The Subtleties of Scientific Style*.

This excerpt is included for your amusement and thoughtful pondering. It also provides a large text that illustrates the effects of formatting are.

What readability and pacing principles from the book up to now show up in this excpert? How do they affect how easy or hard it is to read the content? Discuss at least four points.

1.

2.

3.

4.

Edit the fourth paragraph. What does it mean?

Useful Tools from Microsoft Word

Premium Tip

If you have written with a lot of passive voice, your sentences will tend to be much longer than they have to be, and so the reading will be more difficult.

Turn on the **reading level indicator** under spell check. Aim for a maximum of a Grade 10 reading level – any higher becomes a very difficult academic reading exercise.

There is also a **passive voice indicator.** Eliminate much of the passive voice in your writing with help from Word! Excellent.

CONSISTENCY

Inconsistencies in language in reporting can, and have, resulted in all of the following:

- extra project costs
- returned documents with demands to redo
- confusion within the project team
- confusion in client communications

In school we were taught creative writing and were supposed to use many different words to describe a tree, or the sky, or the river.

In technical writing, do the opposite. Your reader has enough to understand just in the science or engineering or business concepts you present. They do not need to be entertained by varying words.

In fact, regulatory bodies will insist on consistency in terminology. Choose one term for a thing, and keep it.

Premium Tip

Style Sheets

To ensure that everyone on a project team uses the same terminology, capitalization, and spellings, develop a style sheet for each project. Make sure that the client agrees with the terminology, and make sure that everyone on the team has a copy of the style sheet and understands that they are expected to follow it.

Whichever style decisions you make, whether dictated by the client or based on known style guides, be consistent.

The client may not really care whether you capitalize Air Quality Study or not, but they will notice if you capitalize it differently and call it different terms because they'll waste time trying to determine if all of them mean the same thing or you mean different things.

Below is a real example – a regulatory body actually did reject an application that had these inconsistent terms. Pick one term and one capitalization, and keep it!

- Air Quality Study
- the air quality project
- the air quality study
- the air study

Consistency in formatting also helps the reader read your document quickly and comfortably. Confusion is uncomfortable and difficult. Don't do that to your reader. Keep it clear and smooth and easy.

Style Sheets

A wiki page is easy to set up and can provide an easy place to create a project-specific page to keep track of terms and spellings over multiple teams in multiple offices over multiple years.

Consider the solution of a wiki page if you have a geographically distant team. Even if you all work in the same office, having an online wiki can make it easy to keep a central and easily updated location for your style documents. It is key that all team members know how to access this at all times, and that they all understand the importance of following it.

Consistency includes:

- format
- capitalization
- terminology (make sure it is consistent within a document and with what your reader knows)
- spelling (mainly decided by the dictionary, perhaps with some client-specific exceptions)
- details (e.g. discussions with clients, decisions about the project)

Here are some links to publicly available examples of style sheets. As you can see, they include **every detail** that other members of the team might get confused about.

Style sheets can be insanely extensive, which might make sense if you have an international team working on a publishing project.

For a consulting firm with a local project, you may be able to make some assumptions and use short style sheets. If you have an international team or many people new to the client, site, or project, you may wish to use a more extensive one.

http://www.kokedit.com/files/KOK_stylesheet_academic.pdf
http://www.kokedit.com/files/KOK_stylesheet_medical.pdf
https://www.prismnet.com/~tcm/etwr2379/guides/stylesheets.html

RIDICULOUSLY LONG WORDS AND OTHER DISPOSABLES

Short and Simple Language for Clean Clear Writing

At universities and in high school English classes, there is sometimes a perception that whoever uses the longest or most words looks smartest. However, in industry, whoever makes the client happiest looks best!

Math is a simple language. Here's a nice logical if-then statement for you:

> **If** the document is easy
> > for your client to digest
>
> **Then** they will think
> > that you are brilliant.

Achieve this by:
- using short words
- using fewer words
- surrounding important words with white space

Use Fewer Words

There are some words that you can search in a document to discover wordy phrases. "Of" and "for" and "as" often appear in these unnecessarily long phrases. Normally when I find one case of a wordy habit, I hunt through the rest of the document to get rid of it.

This list is actually only a tiny excerpt of a list of more than 20 pages of these phrases. It's possible to build a macro to streamline your documents with the strike of a key. You can find some of these macros free on the internet.

Table 1: Concise Words and Phrases

Inflated Extra-Wordy Language	Concise Language
a certain number of	some
a considerable amount of	much
a considerable number of	many
a decreased amount of	less
a decreased number of	fewer
accounted for by the fact that	because
already exist	exist
alternative choices	choices
an adequate amount of	enough
an example of this is the fact that	for example
annual basis	annually

any and all	any
as a consequence	so
as a result of	because
as is well known	[remove]
as well as	and
as yet	yet
bring to a conclusion	end, close, conclude
by the use of	with
come to an agreement	agree
compared with	than
conduct an investigation	study
considering the fact that	because
contributing factor	factor
do an inspection of	inspect
during such time	while
each and every	each or every, but not both
end result	result
excessive number	too many
for the preparation of	to prepare
for the purpose of	to
for the reason that	because
foreign import	import
from the time that	since
furnish a solution	solve
give encouragement to	encourage
give rise to	cause
group together	group
has been engaged in a study of	has studied
has been shown to be	is
has been widely acknowledged as	is
has the ability	can
have a concern	care, worry
have an effect on	affect, influence
in a northeast direction	northeast
in consequence	so
in consequence of this fact	therefore
in height	high, tall

in length	long
in light of the fact that	because
in only a small number of cases	rarely
in order to	to
in regard to	about
in the neighbourhood of	near, about
is of the opinion	believes
it appears that	apparently
it has been reported by Smith	Smith reported
it has long been known that	[do not use]
it is important to note that	[remove]
it is recommended	
[that consideration be given to]	I/we recommend
it is requested	please
it may, however, be noted that	but
lacks the ability to	cannot
located in immediate vicinity of	near
majority of	most
make an assumption that	assume
new development	development
not ⬚orre⬚t	in⬚orre⬚t
not in a position to	unable to, cannot
notwithstanding the fact that	although
obtained from	of
occurring in connection with	caused by
of an indefinite nature	indefinite
on an annual basis	annually
on behalf of	for, backed, supported
on condition that	if
on most occasions	usually
on the part of	for
owing to the fact that	because
per diem	daily, daily allowance
per⬚or⬚ an assess⬚ent o⬚	assess
potentially dangerous	unsafe, dangerous
potentially hazardous	unsafe, hazardous
presents a picture similar to	resembles

presents a summary	summarizes
previous to	before
prior experience	experience
prior to	before
prior to the occasion when	before
provide a description of	describe
pursuant to	under, about, following
should it prove to be the case that	if
significant portion	most
so as to be able to	to
standards and criteria	standards
start off	start
still remains	remains
storm event	storm
such time as	when
sufficient number	enough
take into consideration	consider
the vast majority of	most
to all appearances	apparently
undertake an analysis	analyze
was found to be	was
while at the same time	while
within a comparatively short period	soon
within the realm of possibility	possible

Use Simple Words

Simple words optimize your chances of getting your readers (our clients) to understand.

You may not always want to aim for the maximum simplicity, but if a chunk of text is especially technical, dense, and hard to read, consider replacing some of the long, dense words with simpler ones.

A note on jargon: people who learned English in India, England, Singapore, and other parts of the old British Empire are sometimes more likely to use complex language. North Americans are more insistent on streamlining and modernizing English than other nations.

Likewise, if you are working on an international report with one of those destinations, ask a local to read over your report to make sure that you have not used local North American language that might not make sense in the international context.

Premium Tip

Clean and Simple Shows You Know

People who are experienced with reading reports note that writers who are confident in a clear strong message use a minimum of complex words, inflated language, and passive voice. They simply say very clearly what they have to say, and that inspires client and reader confidence.

Complex, inflated, passive language is often a sign of flimsy content that experienced readers will see through and be frustrated with quite quickly.

Pare down your language and just say what you know.

Table 2: Simpler Word Choices

Complex	Simple
aforesaid	as previously mentioned
albeit	although, but
approximately	about
apprise	inform
ascertain	find out, learn, check
attached herewith is	here is
authorize	approve
characterize	describe
cognizant	aware
commence	begin, start
demonstrate	show
detrimental	harmful
downsize	reduce
encounter	find
endeavour	try
equivalent	equal
excessive	too much
effectuate	bring about
enumerate	list
etc.	Do not use. Either say that the list "includes" x, y, z, or provide the complete list.
eventuate	result
evidenced	shown, showed

expiration	end, close, finish
finalize	complete, conclude
forthwith	immediately
facilitate	help, ease
finalize	complete, finish, end
frequently	often
future plans	plans
illustration	example
implement	do, set up, begin, carry out
indicate	show, suggest
in the ballpark	about, around
major thrust	the main reason, principal concern, objective
methodology	method
modification	change
necessitate	require, demand, force, compel, call for
obviate	avoid, eliminate
optimum	best
partially	partly
preventative	preventive
prioritize	rank
regarding	about
subsequent	next
sufficient	enough
utilize, utilization	use
vicinity	near, close
spell out	explain, specify, describe, detail
time frame	period, interval, timespan
ultimate	last, final, eventual
utilize	use
whereas	as, since, while
whether	if
worst-case scenario	conservative scenario, worst case, at worst

Other Ways to Simplify

1. Turn Backward Sentences Forward

Sentences sometimes get written backward. This usually requires more words and is harder to understand than simply flipping the sentence around to make it simpler.

If you have to stop and think about a sentence, there may be ways to make it simpler by switching it back to front.

These sentences are often written in the passive voice. Changing them so that they are written in the active voice may solve the problem.

It is also a good idea to lead with the most important information.

NOTE: It can help to get an extra person to help you spot these differences, as they are not always simple to see but are often a relief to see fixed.

Exercise 9

Fix this sentence: *The horse was ridden by the man.*

2. Deflate Longenated Words

Look for nouns (e.g., comparison, presentation, selection) that are formed from verbs (e.g., compare, present, select). In particular, beware of words that end in -al, -ance, -ate, -ion, -ive, -ize and –able.

These are often another clue that you have been using the passive voice, so if you rewrite the sentence in the active voice these words will usually shorten.

Reconsider any ending tacked onto an otherwise simple word. Adding suffixes to verbs slows down reading and hides the action. Rewriting the sentence will make it shorter and more concise.

You can often shorten sentences and make reading easier by taking these parts of words off. For example, instead of "the conclusion was reached…" you could write "we concluded." Here are some other examples:

longenated word	better word	even better word
rationalization	rationale	reason, purpose
implementation	implement	do (v), tool (n)
utilization	utilize	use

This reduces the length of the individual word, and it usually shortens the rest of the sentence as well, as you can eliminate the extra verbs when you reduce the long noun.

3. Simplify with the Judicious Use of Symbols

Other ways to make the text shorter might include thinking like a mathematician: use a few authorized symbols.

- Instead of using the word "degree," use the symbol.

- Instead of "from 90 kilometres to 120 kilometres" you could write "from 90 to 120 km."

Premium Tip

Unauthorized Symbols

Not all symbols in text make it better. For example, "%" is not a word. It is a symbol that follows a number, just like a unit. It is fine to write "There was 63% compliance" but not to write "The % of incident light…" If you are writing a sentence, write a sentence. Do not stick symbols in it (except for measurement units).

Symbols may occasionally be okay in tables, where we sometimes use a shortened style due to space restrictions.

Exercise 10

Make some notes about how symbols are used in your group, here. Are there any conventions or difficulties to be aware of?

CLEAR THE CLOUDS: JARGON AND ACRONYMS

There are two cloudy habits that are common in business and technical writing: jargon and acronyms. To make our reports and communications clear for clients and the public, we need to shine some sun on these clouds and blow them away.

Jargon

- Jargon can facilitate fast technical communications between technical people.
- Acronyms and jargon block communication, just like a cloud over your meaning.
- Jargon has no place in your communications – unless you explain it (then it's no longer jargon).

> **Premium Tip**
>
> **Is it Jargon?**
> Whether a word is jargon or not depends on its familiarity to the audience.

Diagnosis: How to Recognize Jargon

If you are not sure if you have jargon in your writing, ask someone who is outside your usual working group to read it, and ask them if they understand it. Ask them to circle any words that they do not exactly understand or would like further explanation about.

Cure: How to Eliminate Jargon

Jargon is in-crowd language. You want your clients to feel like they *are* part of your inner circle, not that they are standing on the outside while the technical people are in a football huddle with their back to the clients. The way to bring clients into your inner circle where jargon is concerned is simply to make sure that you explain it thoroughly yet simply the first time you use it.

When you do that, the client is brought into your in-crowd, and you can carry on with your discussion.

But what if you are using terms that are difficult to explain to lay people, you ask? Well, then you need to get some help translating it into layperson speak. Certainly it is possible. Recognize when you need to seek outside help and get it from someone outside your group before you start sending reports or talking to the client.

Acronyms

Use acronyms thoughtfully, and only if the acronym makes the text easier to understand somehow. Do not toss them in willy-nilly.

Rules for acronyms:

1. **Eliminate** any abbreviations used less than three times (by spelling out the words).

2. **Define** the others at first use, and perhaps again if the document is long.

3. **Consider** making an acronym list.

A great tool for acronym assessment is called PerfectIt.

http://www.intelligentediting.com/

Premium Tip

Smart Consistency Software: PerfectIt

This magical little program is a lot of help when you want to tune up your documents before sending them to clients. It will tell you all of the following things:

1. when you have spelled a word two ways

2. when you have not spelled out an acronym at first use

3. when you have not spelled out numbers consistently

4. when you have used an acronym for two different things

5. it will make you an acronym list

6. and if you want some other feature, ask Daniel, the developer, and he might just draft it up for you. He's a nice guy.

Example: A Properly Used Acronym

In the paragraph below, the acronym SAGD is used correctly.

> *We currently have two major producing steam assisted gravity drainage (SAGD) projects in the oil sands. Foster Creek is one of the largest and considered among the best commercial and technical SAGD projects in the industry. It has the distinction of being the first commercial SAGD oil operation in Alberta.*

This acronym:

- Reduces the volume of the paragraph significantly.

- Is defined properly at first use.

- Is used many more times in the document.

Example: An Improperly Used Acronym

> **Step 2: Use elegant words**
>
> - As in fashion, elegant = simple.
> - To **impress our high school teachers**, we learned big, complex words.
> - To **impress clients**, keep it simple (KIS).

This acronym (KIS in the screen shot):
- does not reduce the word count of this material
- adds clutter to the page
- is not used at all in the rest of the document
- adds nothing to the reader's understanding of the material

Allowed Shorthand Method: Defining Parties

Often we use a shorthand for companies or parties in a document. This reduces the tedium of reading long names, which is good.

For example, a law firm might be called Wytryschowski, Pullin, Bobkle, and Daughter, but it would be ridiculous to have to spell out a company name that takes more than half a line, more than once. Therefore at the first use, you write something like this: "The attorney of record for this project is Wytryschowski, Pullin, Bobkle, and Daughter (WPBD)," and then when you refer to the firm again, you can use just WPBD.

You might also use just the main name of the company. For example, Davor Hydraulic Services Inc. might be introduced as follows: "Davor Hydraulic Services, Inc. (Davor), is providing all of the irrigation on this project." Then for the rest of the document you need only call the company Davor.

Note: Do not define parties in all capital letters. Use Davor, not DAVOR. All capital letters should be reserved for acronyms. Words in all capital letters are distracting to the eye in a report. It is harder to read pages that have many words in all capital letters.

CAPITALIZATION

Capitalization is a more important nuance than you may think. Whether a word is capitalized or not gives the reader clues about what kind of a word it is.

General words not capitalized	Specific words: capitalized
Examples: directions (north, south), all nouns, verbs, and adjectives that are not names, numbers, general cases of any of the named items in the right column.	Capitalize all proper names, trade names, government departments and agencies of government, job titles, names of associations, companies, clubs, religions, languages, nations, races, places, and addresses.
Example:	
The Canadian government department in charge of food safety is called The Canadian Food Inspection Agency.	

Communicate the Capitalization, and Do It in Writing
The tiny issue of capitalization eats up many hours of people at all levels. Be efficient and reduce the misery. For each project and/or client, create a list of which words are to be capitalized and not capitalized. This will save time and headaches later on. Distribute the list widely. Make sure everyone has access to it.

Premium Tip

A good source for the capitalization and spelling of geographic features in Canada is *The Canadian Style,* available for free online through the government web page.

http://www.btb.termiumplus.gc.ca/tcdnstyl-chap?lang=eng&lettr=chapsect15&info0=15#zz15

Capitalization of Numbered Items in a Document or on a Site (tables, sections, figures, facilities, features)

If something is one of many items, or is a general description, you do not capitalize it. Capitalize items that are names of specific items that you can point to.

"Figure 2" is the name of a certain figure, just like "Sally" is the name of a certain woman. Whenever you have a numbered item such as a table, figure, step, or even physical feature, if you can point to the specific one named by that number, then capitalize it.

Examples: Table 2, Figure 8, Step 3, Outlet 4, Pipeline 5, Lake 2

Capitalization of Site Features

As with numbered items, capitalize features of a site when they are specific names of a specific feature. Do not capitalize them if they are general terms.

For example, there are four dykes on the site. They are called Dyke 1, North Dyke, Dyke 2, and West Dyke.

If you are saying, "we checked the north dyke," and the north dyke is not officially called the north dyke, but just happens to be the as-yet-un-named dyke at the north end of the site, then there might be a case for not capitalizing it.

Biology

Use the common name the first time you use scientific names, to make your report easy to understand. Put scientific names in parentheses, italicize them, and do not underscore. Write thegenus, species, and (if appropriate) subspecies. Capitalize the genus and lowercase the species and subspecies.

Spell out the genus the first time. After that, you may use the first letter followed by a period when naming the same or other species later in the text. The abbreviation used for the genus must be clear.

Example: All sightings of barred owls *(Strix varia)* and spotted owls *(S. occidentalis)* occurred at night.

When referring to multiple or unknown species within a single genus, use the following abbreviations:

- Multiple species of one genus: *spp.*

  ☼ Huckleberries (Vaccinium spp.) were the dominant component of the shrub layer.

- Unknown species: *sp.*

  ☼ Pitfall trapping resulted in the capture of a single, unidentified shrew *(Sorex sp.)*.

- Multiple subspecies of one species: *ssp.*

  ☼ Three subspecies of the common garter snake *(Thamnophis sirtalis ssp.)* are present in the project area.

Geography

As with any noun in English, only capitalize it if it is part of a specific name and becomes a proper name.

e.g. The mountain over there is named Pigeon Mountain.

(general noun = mountain; proper noun = Pigeon Mountain)

Do not capitalize north, south, east, and west, unless they are part of a name.

Capitalize specific geographical regions and features: Western Canada, the North, High Arctic, Prairies, Canadian Shield, Rocky Mountains. Use lowercase for regions not generally known as specific geographic areas, such as southern Alberta, and for geographic descriptions, such as arctic winds or western Canadian.

Other

Hyphenated terms in titles. In titles for which the format is to use initial caps, lowercase words that follow a hyphen:

- *Hatchery-related Fishery Effects on Salmon*

Occupations. Do not capitalize job titles (general manager, project manager, division director, etc.) in text unless they precede a person's name. When they precede the name, there is no comma separating the title and the person's name.

- *Division Director Alicia Marriot*

- *Alicia Marriot, division director*

Proper nouns. Capitalize nouns that constitute unique identification (the name of) for a specific person, place, or thing:

- *Praveen Kulkarni*
- *Bow River*
- *Oldman Dam*

Do not capitalize job titles (general manager, project manager, division director, etc.) in text unless they precede a person's name. When they precede the name, there is no comma separating the title and the person's name.

Proper names. Capitalize common names when they are an integral part of the full name of a specific person, place, or thing (i.e., when they are proper nouns/names). Where the government rather than the place is meant, the words state, city, and the like are usually capitalized.

city	City of Montreal
lake	Lake Tahoe
river	Saskatchewan River
state	Arizona State

Titles

Capitalize formal titles when used immediately before a name. Use lowercase formal titles when they stand alone or occur in constructions that set them off from a name by commas:

- *We submitted the report to Professor R. Loveness for her review.*
- *We submitted the report to Dr. Richa Loveness, a professor at the university, for her review.*

Unauthorized Capitalization

Overcapitalizing seems to be a fairly common human tendency.

In Victorian times, capitalizing Every Important Word was very common. In handwritten letters, capitalizing words was a way to convey Important Events and Extreme Emotion such as True Love.

In German, all nouns are capitalized.

However, in modern English, capitalizing too many words is inappropriate and does not lead to clarity. Capitalized words are distracting.

Tribal throwback

Sometimes when a group of people work together all the time, however, they start to think certain words are Really Important. These end up becoming a jargon of their own.

Premium Tip

Client preferences

If your clients, in their own tribal way, generate Important Capitalized Words and insist on capitalizing them, fine. Just make sure that you write down those words in the style list and communicate them to the rest of the team.

POTENTIALLY TROUBLESOME WORDS (LEGALLY SPEAKING)

Certain words imply serious responsibility, and if you use them casually, you can get in big trouble if a project goes awry.

Example

What kind of responsibility?

Consider this contractual statement: "Consultant assumes responsibility for all injury of any kind or nature whatsoever, whether directly or indirectly resulting from acts or omissions of Consultant...regardless if such injury is contributed by the sole negligence of Client..."

Instead, say: "Consultant assumes responsibility for injury, including death and damage to property, caused by its negligent acts or omissions as respects services performed by the Consultant under this Contract."

Consider how word meanings vary. For each word, there can be differences between the following four aspects of meaning.

- the special meaning you intended
- the dictionary definition
- the layman's meaning
- professional liability implications

When deciding whether a word is safe to use or not, consider whether, if things go wrong, the judge is clearly going to understand the meaning you intended when you wrote your documents.

The following list includes some words and phrases that fall under this category.

Ask!

If you are not sure of anything, ask. Your colleagues would rather discuss important issues with you before it goes to the client, than struggle along with you if something happens and they end up needing to support you in court!

Premium Tip

Table: Risky Words

acceptable	every	occasional
all	everywhere, everyday, everybody, everyone, and everything	of any kind or nature
always	examination	oversee
any	extremely	percent
appropriate	final	possible
approve	free	potential
arising out of	full	prevent
assure	good chance	probable/probably
at least	guarantee	properly
best	howsoever	readily
certify, certified, certification	ideal	representative
complete	in whole or in part	require
control	inevitable	resulting from
could	inspect	safe
critical	inspect/inspection	safety
define	insure	shall
determine	least	should
direct (the verb)	likely	significant
directly or indirectly	maximum/maximize	sole negligence
economical	minimum/minimize	sufficient
economically feasible	monitor	thorough
elevated	most	total
eliminate	must	unsafe
empty	necessary	warrant
ensure	never, no, no one, none, nothing, nowhere	whole
entire	not greater than	whomsoever
equal	not less than	will
	not more than	will be required
essential	obvious, obviously	worst

Premium Tip

Dangerous Descriptions – Just the Facts, Ma'am
Precise statement of numbers is clear, factual, truthful, and therefore a good practice.
Beware which descriptive words you use. It is the adjectives that can really get you into trouble.

It also pays to be aware of your use of adjectives and adverbs, as these are often subjective and can lead to misunderstandings.

Instead of saying, for example, that the concrete was allowed to dry "slowly," which is not very definite or clear, say exactly what you did do.

"The concrete slab was allowed to dry over a period of 48 hours. A person on-site watered the concrete each 8 hours to slow the rate of drying."

Being precise is important.

One senior environmental scientist remarks wryly that young environmental scientists often get excited and want to use the word "significant" when they can see a result, for example in a difference in nutrient measurements in a stream in two different seasonal measurements.

However, the idea of a "significant difference" in the nutrient values of a stream is quite alarming to clients, the public, and potential environmental lobbyist readers. A nutrient difference from season to season is completely normal in streams. So while the difference may well be a significant difference, you want to be careful about implying any sort of disaster in your report.

The term "significant" usually has quantitative values attached to it and, like the other risky words, such terms should be discussed with your supervisor before you include them.

TRICKY ENGLISH WORDS (FOR SPELLING AND USAGE)

Here are some terms that are commonly misused.

Table: Commonly Misused Words

Confused Words	Definition
a lot allot	**A lot** means many. (Note: "Alot" is non-standard English and must not be used.) **Allot** means to distribute something.
accept except	**Accept** is a verb that means agree with, take in, or receive. *(The client will accept the report once the changes have been made.)* **Except** is a preposition that means apart from. *(Everyone except Bob is going to the presentation.)*
advance advanced	**Advance** describes a forward position in place and time. *(She prepared the advance change notice.)* **Advanced** means at a late stage or at a high level. *(She received an advanced degree from McGill University.)*
advise advice	**Advise** is a verb meaning to recommend. *(We were advised of the risks.)* **Advice** is a noun that means an opinion or a recommendation. *(I would like to ask for your advice on this matter.)*
affect effect	**Affect** (verb) means to influence or change something. *(The construction method will affect project costs.)* **Effect** (noun) means result. *(The effect on project costs will be small.)* **Effect** (verb) means to cause [something] to be. *(to effect a change)*
all ready already	**All ready** means entirely ready or everyone is ready. *(We are all ready to begin the test.)* **Already** means by this time. *(The preliminary work has already been done.)*
among between	**Among** refers to more than two things. *(A strong feeling of loyalty grew among the club members.)* **Between** usually refers to only two things. *(There is little difference between the two results.)*
bring take	**Bring** means to carry from a distant place to a nearer place. *Bring* is about coming: If the object is coming here, someone is *bringing* it. **Take** means to carry from a nearer place to a more distance place. *Take* is about going: If the object is going there, someone is *taking* it.

Confused Words	Definition
Can may	**Can** denotes ability. *(The spillway can be accessed from either end of the dam.)* **May** denotes permission. *(Contractors may access the site from the south gate only.)*
common mutual	**Common** means belonging to or shared by two or more individuals or by all members of a group. *(The buildings share a common parking lot.)* **Mutual** means directed by each toward the other, or having the same feelings one for the other. *(The editors reached a mutual agreement to work overtime.)*
complementary complimentary	**Complementary** describes things or people that go together well (i.e., they complete each other). **Complimentary** means expressing praise. **Complimentary** also describes an item given without charge.
compose comprise	**Compose** means to create or to put together. *(The health and safety team is composed of eight safety engineers.)* **Comprise** means include or contain. *Comprise* should never be followed by "of." *(The proposals team comprises four technical professionals and three managers.)* **Caution:** Avoid *comprise*. Because of widespread misunderstanding of the correct use of this word, authors run the risk of having their writing changed from correct to incorrect.
continual continuous	**Continual** means repeated again and again. *(The system failed continually.)* **Continuous** means uninterrupted. *(The electroencephalogram will record brainwaves continuously for an hour.)*
criterion criteria	**Criterion** is singular. *(His only criterion for success was how much money he made.)* **Criteria** is plural. *(She had three criteria for a meaningful life: to love well, to make life better for others, and to leave an enduring and meaningful legacy behind her.)*
data datum	**Data** has traditionally taken the plural because in Latin data is the plural of **datum**. Many authoritative sources recognize both "data is" and "data are" as correct.
definitely defiantly	**Definitely** means for certain. **Defiantly** means to act with an attitude of rebellion.
discreet discrete	**Discreet** means circumspect. **Discrete** means having separate parts.

Confused Words	Definition
e.g. i.e.	**e.g.** means for example (Latin: exempli gratia) and is followed by an example. **i.e.** means "that is" (Latin: id est) and is followed by an explanation.
farther further	**Farther** is used for physical distance. **Further** is used to extend an explanation.
fewer less	**Fewer** refers to items that can be counted. Use **less** for mass nouns or amounts, as in less information or less vegetation. See also many/much.
historical historic	Historical means having taken place in history. (The historical records are kept in the vault.) Historic means having significance in history. (The first trip to the moon was a historic event.)
in situ	*In situ* is Latin for *in place*. Since it is Latin, it is usually italicized. Some industry personnel perceive that it is so common that they do no italicize it. Do not hyphenate this pharse, even when **in situ** is used as a modifier. *(In situ tests are preferred.)*
inter- intra-	**Inter-** means between or among, as in international, which means between or among nations. **Intra-** means within, as in intracranial, which means within the skull.
it's its	**It's** is a contraction of "it is." Avoid contractions in formal writing. *(It's a beautiful day.)* **Its** is a possessive pronoun. *(The contractor is responsible for compliance with the health and safety plan by its employees and subcontractors.)*
li☐en☐e li☐ense	A **licence** (noun) is a certificate, tag or document in Canada. **License** (verb) mean to grant or give a licence. In the US, license is spelled with an "s" whether it's a noun or a verb. Likewise, in Canada, "practice" is the preferred spelling for the noun and "practise" is the preferred spelling for the verb, but in the US, it's "practise" for both noun and verb.
lose loose	**Lose** mean to be deprived of. **Loose** means not fastened.`
many much	**Many** modifies countable nouns. *(Many Americans travel to Europe.)* **Much** modifies uncountable nouns. *(They have much money in the bank.)* See also fewer/less.

Confused Words	Definition
⯑e myself I	Use **"I"** when you are the subject (actor); use **"me"** when you are the object (receiver); use **"myself"** (reflexive) only when you have performed or will perform that action yourself, or when I is already the subject of the sentence. Use of **myself** in pla⯑e o⯑I or **me** is not grammatically correct, even in compound subjects. Some people seem to believe it sounds fancier to say "myself," but actually it just sounds like you're trying to use longer words. Not good.
method methodology	**Methodology** is the study or discussion of method. *Methodology* is commonly and incorrectly used as a pretentious synonym for *method*.
⯑etre ⯑eter	A **metre** is a unit of measurement in Canadian and British spelling. A **meter** is a measuring device. In the US, the unit of measurement is also spelled this way
prin⯑ipal prin⯑iple	**Principal** means chief or most important. **Principle** means basic truth or rule.
quiet quite	**Quiet** means without sound. **Quite** is an adjective that is rarely required in technical writing.
stationary stationery	**Stationary** means not moving. **Stationery** is writing materials.
then than	**Then** is mainly an adverb, often used to show a time sequence. *(First we conduct the study and then we write the report.)* **Than** is mainly a conjunction used in making comparisons. *(A highway is wider than a sidewalk.)*
toward towards	**Toward** and **towards** are equally acceptable in Canada. **Toward** is preferred in the United States. Outside North America, **towards** is more common.

INTERNATIONAL SPELLING

"If the English language made any sense, a catastrophe would be an apostrophe with fur."
– cartoonist Doug Larson

Consistent spelling is important to avoid misunderstandings and even potential liability. To reduce conflict around spellings, choose one dictionary and stick with it unless there are documented reasons for variations. Consistent spelling standards will save time for the whole team.

Dictionaries for Canada, the US, and international regions are suggested in the reference section at the front of this booklet. Typically, use spellings for the destination of the document preferentially over the region where the document is written.

Premium Tip

Microsoft Word's Magic Wrongenation Function

Microsoft Word has many useful tools, but it also creates many errors. If you think that the grammar in a sentence is correct, do not change it just because Word has a green underline under your sentence. Sometimes Word suggests that there is an error when there is no error at all.

If you think you might have an error but you are not sure, ask another human being or check with the designated dictionary (e.g. Canadian Oxford) before fiddling with the text just to get Word to make the little green or red squiggle go away.

Check that your Microsoft Word is set to Canadian English if you are in Canada, US English while in the US, and so on. There are many options.

You can customize the spell check dictionary to add words. This is particularly useful for high-level scientific words, which are often missing, and names.

American

American spelling is the default MS Word spell check dictionary. However, a higher-authority source than that is Merriam-Webster's Dictionary, www.m-w.com, if there is any uncertainty about:

- punctuation
- spa⬚in⬚
- hyphenation
- spellin⬚

American spelling differs from Canadian and Commonwealth spelling in words that include:

US: center, meter, fiber, favor, color, neighbor, labor, vapor, organize, modeling, traveling, gray, sulfur, and catalog

UK/Canada: centre, metre, fibre, favour, colour, neighbour, labour, vapour, organise (UK), modelling, travelling, grey, sulphur, catalogue.

Canadian and Commonwealth Spelling

If you receive a report that has been through Canada or Europe, it might be helpful for you to have information about the spelling habits. Here are a few common classifications of differences between American and Commonwealth spelling.

Table: Canadian Spelling

Type	Example
verbs ending in ise/ize	⬚se *ize*, so analyze, organize, maximize/ minimize
nouns ending in our/or	⬚se *our*, so colour, favourable, neighbour
nouns ending in re/er	⬚se *re*, so centre, kilometre (but meter for an instrument e.g., pH meter)
single l/double l to add suffixes to wor	⬚se *ll,* so fuelling/fuelled, modelling/ modelled, travelling/travelled
nouns ending in ce/se	⬚se *-ce*, for the nouns licence, defence, and practice, and use *-se* for the verbs practise and license

British

British English uses -ise instead of -ize, but is otherwise quite similar to Canadian.

One major difference is in punctuation. The British use "wow", with the comma or period outside the quotation marks.

American and Canadian style is to put the comma or period inside the quotation marks, like this: "Trust me," she said, "it's all true."

BASIC SCIENTIFIC NUMERACY

When to Use Numbers

- Use numerals instead of words with units, dates, and symbols (13.4 m, February 8, 16%)

- Use numerals for numbers in highways, time, and addresses.

- Numerals can be used at the beginning of bullets if the bullet is not a sentence. Numbers that start a sentence are normally spelled out instead of written as numerals.

- Many style guides used to spell out all numbers less than ten. The Chicago Manual of Style still recommends this, however, the most recent version of Scientific Style and Format suggests that for science and engineering papers, it might be just as appropriate to use numerals all the time, even for 0 and 1.

Premium Tip

Lay Down the Law and Don't Be a Sissy
Make decisions about rules for numbers within your group or company. Write them down in the style guide. Enforce them. This will save you so much time and hassle, you will wonder why you didn't do it years ago.

Punctuating Numbers

- Always use a full space between the quantity and the unit. Do not put hyphens before metric units, not even when used as adjectives (this differs from Imperial style. A 12-foot board is a 2.4 m board).

- Use a "hard space" (shift + ctrl + space) between the quantity and symbol if you want to make sure they are not separated at a line break.

- Check that numbers cited in the text match those given in tables.

- Should you put a comma in numbers over 999, or not? Metric standards say to use a space instead. However, the issue has been so rife with conflict that the most recent edition of the Council of Science Editors Style guide recently went backwards on their advice to move toward the metric space, and are again suggesting the comma. If you have international projects, the space is wiser, but consider your readership, clients, colleagues, and market.

Eight Style Points for Metric Measurements

Certain style points for metric are different from the Imperial measurement system. Though some style guides may continue to follow the historical style for decades to come, here we would like to set the record straight and clarify the correct styles, according to international metric standards.

1. Put a space before a metric unit.

This includes all metric units. Use 99 m, not 99m. (This is often done incorrectly in news media, but that does not make it acceptable in scientific papers. Use the correct convention rather than mimicking others' errors.)

This convention extends to degrees of temperature. Add a space before degrees Celsius (°C). For example, use 32 °C, not 32°C.

Note: For Fahrenheit, most people would omit the space. That is still acceptable if you are writing degrees Fahrenheit. When you write in Celsius, use a space.

2. Do not put hyphens before metric units, not even in an adjectival sense.

In the Imperial system, hyphens between numbers and units were (and are) common. This is not recommended metric practice, though it has persisted in Canadian use.

So while you might write six-inch nails, or even 6-inch nails, they would be 15 cm nails in metric, not 15-cm nails. It might be a 6-mile run, but it is a 10 km run. Think of it as less romantic if you must, but do not put hyphens before metric units.

3. The case of the letters for the metric symbols matters very much, so get it right.

Mm means megametres, or one million (1 000 000) m, while mm means millimetres, or one-thousandth (0.001) m.

4. Do not put a period after the symbol for a metric unit.

The only time there would be a period following a metric unit would be if it was at the end of a sentence.

5. Do not add an "s" to make metric units plural. They are plural already.

E.g. 1 m, 2 m, not 2 ms, as ms would mean milliseconds.

6. For modern metric measurement, signal units of area with an exponent of 2 for square units, and units of volume with an exponent of 3 for cubed units.

E.g. m^2, m^3.

A common error that authors leave in manuscripts is not to check that their superscripts are formatted properly; "m2'" does not mean metres squared; it must be m^2.

The units litre (L) for volume and hectare (ha) for area have been approved for use with the standard SI units of m3 and m2.

7. Never put metric units in italic type.

Letters in italics are variables. Metric prefixes should be set in plain type.

8. Choose metric prefixes that will be easily known to your reader, while making the number as easy as possible.

The most commonly known prefixes are kilo- and milli-. Since the advent of computers, people have become more familiar with tera-, giga-, and mega-. Since the advent of microbiology and nanotechnology, people have become more familiar with micro- and nano-. But have a thought for your readers before getting too fancy.

A full list of metric prefixes is available from *The Canadian Style* online on Termium, at http://www.btb.termiumplus.gc.ca/tcdnstyl-srch?lang=eng&srchtxt=metric+prefixes&i=1&cur=1&nmbr=14&comencsrch.x=0&comencsrch.y=0

While choosing a familiar prefix, also make the number as easy as possible (usually between 0.1 and 1000).

Example:

Rather than describing a distance as 12 dam or 1.2 hm, write it as 120 m. It is better to use whole numbers than decimal numbers less than one, so 120 m is better than 0.12 km, unless for some reason this number is being compared with a number of other distances expressed in km. It is also better to use common prefixes instead of the rarer ones, which may not be known. Everyone knows m and km and cm and mm, but fewer people would recognize hm, dam, and dm, much less remember what factor of ten the prefix goes with.

Only one symbol can be used with each metric unit.

Symbol and Keyboard Shortcuts

Keyboard shortcuts that can be used to speed up your writing or insert proper symbols are listed in Table 3.

Table 4: Keyboard Shortcuts

CTRL+C	Copy
CTRL+X	Cut
CTRL+V	Paste
CTRL+Z	Undo
CTRL+B	Bold
CTRL+U	Underline
CTRL+I	Italics
CTRL+F	Find
CTRL + Shift + space bar	Non-breaking space
CTRL + Shift + Hyphen	Non-breaking hyphen
CTRL + equals button	Subscript (e.g., SO_4^{2-})
CTRL + Shift + equals button	Superscript (e.g., m^3)
ALT + 0150	En dash (–)
ALT + 0151	Em dash (—)
ALT + 0181	µ
ALT + 0215	×
ALT + 0247	÷
ALT + 0177	±
ALT + 0186	º
ALT + CTRL + C	©
ALT + CTRL + R	®
ALT + CTRL + T	™

You can also assign a shortcut key to a symbol or special character. See the Microsoft Office Help page.

A complete list of Microsoft Office keyboard shortcuts is available at: http://support.microsoft.com/kb/290938

AUTHOR BIO

Christa Bedwin has 18 years of experience writing, editing, and teaching in industry, government, academia, and educational publishing.

She now teaches engineers, scientists, and business people to communicate better, and helps people to publish books to preserve their knowledge.

Christa was raised on a ranch in the foothills of the Rockies and has travelled extensively. She has a wide range of job and travel experiences and is a dynamic instructor and speaker. Her positive attitude and enthusiasm are contagious.